Poems of Katherine Mansfield

Poems of Katherine Mansfield

Edited by
Vincent O'Sullivan

Auckland
Oxford University Press
Melbourne   Oxford

Oxford University Press

Oxford University Press, Walton Street, Oxford OX2 6DP

OXFORD   NEW YORK   TORONTO
DELHI   BOMBAY   CALCUTTA   MADRAS   KARACHI
PETALING JAYA   SINGAPORE   HONG KONG   TOKYO
NAIROBI   DAR ES SALAAM   CAPE TOWN
MELBOURNE   AUCKLAND
and associated companies in
BERLIN   IBADAN

Oxford is a trade mark of Oxford University Press

First published 1988
Selection and editorial matter © Vincent O'Sullivan 1988
New Katherine Mansfield texts © The Estate of Katherine Mansfield 1988

ISBN 0 19 558192 X   Cloth
ISBN 0 19 558199 7   Paper

Cover designed by Fay McAlpine
Photoset in Bembo by Rennies Illustrations Ltd.,
and printed in Hong Kong
Published by Oxford University Press
1A Matai Road, Greenlane, Auckland 3, New Zealand

Contents

Introduction

I

Within weeks of Katherine Mansfield's death, John Middleton Murry began his work of veneration that led him to publish so much that Mansfield herself never thought of attempting to print. *Poems by Katherine Mansfield*, brought out the next year, was perhaps the single volume that would have caused her particular disquiet. Although she returned to writing verse at different times during her life, Mansfield made no claims to being a poet. Murry was determined to establish her as one. He brought together the twenty-odd poems she had published mostly under pseudonyms, and another fifty from manuscripts that very often were the sketchiest of drafts. He presented as finished or considered work what was not only occasional, but also extremely casual. For Mansfield wrote much of her verse primarily for the moment of expression and often with no desire to revise. The merest jottings such as 'The Town Between the Hills' were consequently elevated by Murry in a grossly misleading way.

Wherever possible, this edition has corrected Murry's cosmetic editing against the original manuscripts or first printings, restoring the spontaneity of her own erratic punctuation, and the frequently off-hand nature of the verse.

I have not included here the mawkish 'Child Verse: 1907', which Murry seized upon as evidence for that rare and childish spirit he was anxious to impose on Mansfield's toughly incisive personality. I have added a number of unpublished and uncollected early vignettes as well as unpublished later poems, which considerably modify that sometimes anaemic image of 'Mansfield the poet' ensured for sixty-five years by Murry's selection. There are a few verses from periodicals and a number in manuscript that I have not included in this selection on the grounds that they are weaker or repetitive examples of kinds already represented.

II

As a young girl and adolescent, Mansfield turned out dozens of negligible verses, and in her twenty months back in Wellington after her time at Queen's College, London, she wrote many specifically for children. She intended publishing these with accompanying sentimental illustrations by a woman friend with whom she was infatuated. The proposed book was dropped when the infatuation ran its course. She did, however, attempt to get the verses into print, trying places as diverse as *Cassell's Magazine*, the *Ladies' Home Journal*, and the *Windsor Magazine*. Only one found its way into the *Lone Hand* (see Notes). Another Australian journal, *Steele Rudd's Magazine*, carried the cryptic message 'K. B. (N.Z.): Sorry unsuitable.'

At much the same time as writing these verses, which she derived rather limply from R. L. Stevenson's *A Child's Garden of Verses* and similar collections, Mansfield turned to a more stimulating source — to the prose poems at the end of Ernest Dowson's *Decorations*, and to the *fin-de-siècle* miniatures of Oscar Wilde. 'This style of work absorbs me, at present' she told an Australian editor in September 1907, although she denied that she had 'cribbed' from her mentors. The tone of her vignettes is calculatedly hectic, flushed with their own daring as they draw on that decadence which, like Joyce in Dublin a few years earlier, Mansfield believed necessary if the provincial was to break through to something more. A process 'towards life through corruption', Joyce had described it in *Stephen Hero*. A 'mad wave . . . of super-aestheticism' was Mansfield's Wellington variant. She hoped that her country might 'become almost decadent . . . for a year or two and then find balance and proportion' (*Collected Letters of Katherine Mansfield*, I, pp. 26, 44). Thus her vignettes, with their emphasis on atmosphere and mood rather than sustained sincerity or event, were not simply a fashionable form. They first proposed to her a freedom that already moved towards the stories she would later write, easing emotion away from the need to account for it fully, allowing an adjectival assault on the notion that one needed to be either consistent or explanatory. They were excursions into that dimly defined territory between the expectations of prose and the freer emotional contours of verse.

Mansfield was back in London in the summer of 1908, liberated from family surveillance and suddenly in love with a young musician. She continued with her prose poems, wrote a number of conventionally melancholy lyrics with her frequent motif of annihilation and loss, and attempted too in 'The Winter Fire' what she called both 'realism' and 'a little cruel' (see *Collected Letters of Katherine Mansfield*, I, pp. 81–3, 84). Here she takes a lead from Arthur Symons' *London Nights*, and something too from such socially earnest and insistent blank verse as John Davidson's 'A Woman and her Son'. An obvious line might be traced from an early poem such as 'The Trio' to Mansfield's later store of deserted or isolated women; those figures who with neither money nor position are obliged to languish or to serve. There is also in the same poem, written during a winter of massive unemployment, a political implication of the kind that Mansfield commentators generally ignore, as they do her few but perceptive remarks on Maoris, her views on the Irish uprising of 1916, her contempt for patriotism during the First World War, and her frequently implied allegiance to working-class qualities rather than bourgeois standards. The myth of the banker's politically inert daughter dies almost as slowly as Murry's exquisite flame.

Mansfield wrote verse spasmodically after 1909. She did not use it again for such declarative statements as her Whitmanesque address to the Polish artist and patriot Stanislaw Wyspiansky. Admiration for an old and troubled nation gave her the moment to think about her own, which was so demonstrably new, comparatively untroubled, indisputably peripheral. For to come from the margins of any culture means defining an absence rather than quarrying a source. One of the interests in reading Mansfield's later prose is to observe that marginality assume the centre.

For the next year or two, Mansfield's verse wore a deliberately Slavic air, as she assigned to 'Boris Petrovsky' most of the poems she contributed to *Rhythm*. Although she answered the editorial demand for brutality and colour — Murry's current prescription for the Modern — with such murder stories as 'Millie' and 'The Woman at the Store', the poems owed rather more to the various vogues of the lonely child, the Celtic seashore, and the post-*symboliste* landscapes of emotive correspondence. But Mansfield clearly thought of her verse as secondary to her main business as a writer. For a short time after her brother's death in 1915, she hoped to commemorate him in elegaic verse, and wrote the series of brief, loosely metred lines that set as simply as she could the quiet, unspectacular memories of their years together in Wellington. When she chanced on her earlier draft of *The Aloe* she realized that prose, of course, would do just that more effectively. At the same time, to while away winter evenings with word games, she wrote as the merest sketches what Murry grouped as the 'Villa Pauline' poems.

In 1918, on holiday in Looe, Mansfield experimented with poems that her painter friend Anne Estelle Rice would accompany with drawings. The plan came to no more than the proposed book of children's verse ten years earlier. Yet the experiment was interesting. Those few poems are almost imagist in their uncluttered matching of a single mood to a single pictorial effect. Soon after writing such pieces as 'Malade', she reworked them into short prose paragraphs. In describing them still as poems, she was as reluctant as in the days of her vignettes to distinguish sharply between the genres. She wrote to Murry, 'They are not in verse or vers libre — I can't do those things' (*Collected Letters of Katherine Mansfield*, II, p. 204). In fact she could. The verse versions from Cornwall were as close as she came to an original poetic form in placing her rhythms in units of phrasing and irregular line length rather than pre-determined feet. They were free too of the tired diction she returned to when she wrote as 'Elizabeth Stanley' the kind of verse that met Murry's editorial taste in the *Athenaeum*.

Mansfield's own preferences in poetry were firmly traditional. For years she carried about with her Sir Arthur Quiller-Couch's *Oxford Book of English Verse*, and her letters and *Journal* return especially to Shakespeare, but also to the Elizabethans, Wordsworth primarily among the Romantics, and Hardy. Among her contemporaries she greatly admired Arthur Waley's translations from the Chinese, found de la Mare admirable, referred obliquely to Edna St Vincent Millay and Robert Frost, castigated Yeats for pomposity, detested Pound on personal grounds, and considered Eliot 'unspeakably dreary' — although in 'Night Scented Stock' she parodies him affectionately. She regarded a great deal of modern verse as 'ever so expensive *pompes funebres*' (*Collected Letters of Katherine Mansfield*, II, p. 318). She was too impressed by Murry's own meagre gifts as a poet to look to the more adventurous or robust possibilities among the living writers she knew and read.

We may regard her poetry now as Mansfield herself tended to think of it — unassuming, often slight, serviceable enough for occasional published excursions into inherited effects and derived styles, yet capable too of unexpectedly inventive turns and intensity. Or we may read it for its vivid biographical facets, the quick clarities of her attention as it catches at angles of memory or self-scrutiny. Certainly there are a number of poems that stand firmly on their own terms: *To Stanislaw Wyspiansky*, 'To L. H. B.', the Cornwall experiments, the late signals of distress when death and the male protector imaginatively coalesce. And always there is the fascination of a great prose writer's mind when for various reasons she chooses to move from her *métier*.

'This is My World'

This is my world, this room of mine
Here I am living — — — & here I shall die
All my interests are here, in fine
— — — The hours slip quickly by.

Look on these shelves — just books, you would say
Friends I can tell you, one & all
Most of them sorrowful — — some of them gay — —
And my pictures that line the wall.

Yes, that is a Doré, from where I sit
At night with my books or my work, I see
The light that falls & glorifies it — — —
And I gaze & it strengthens me.

Ah! in this cupboard, my miser's store
Of music finger it sheaf by sheaf
Elixir of life — — it is something more
It is heaven to me, in brief.

And that is my 'cello, my all in all
Ah, my beloved, quiet you stand
— — — If I let the bow ever so softly fall,
— — — The magic lies under my hand.

And on Winter night & when the fire is low
We comfort each other, till it would seem
That the night outside, all cold & snow
Is the ghost of a long past dream.

This is my world, this room of mine
Here I am living — — — here I shall die
All my interests are here in fine
— — The hours slip quickly by.

The Students' Room

In the students' room the plain & simple beds —
The pictures that line the walls — of various excellence thrown
together
And the students with heads bent low, silent over their books.

Vignette — 'Through the Autumn afternoon'

Through the Autumn afternoon — I sat before the fire in the
Library — and read — almost a little wildly.
I wanted to drug myself with books — drown my thoughts
in a great violet sea of Oblivion.
I read about Youth — how the Young and the Strong had gone
forth into battle — with banners of golden and blue and crimson.
Of the sunshine that turned their processions into a river of
colour — and the songs that — mellow and sweet — rose in
their round throats —
I read of the young Painters — hollow eyed and pale — who
paced their studios like young tigers — and with stupendous
colossal ideas —
How they sat together at night — in sweet companionship —
round a fire — their cigarette smoke — mystical — ethereal.
And in the glowing coals — was shadowed the beautiful —
flame like body of Art.
And deeply I pored over the books of Youthful Musicians.
Splendid — and tragic — and prophetic their faces gleamed
at me — always with that strange haunted look — They had
taken Life to them — and sung a Scarlet Song — that had
no ending and no beginning — And I read of all their resolves
— and of their feverish haste — and the Phantastic Desires
that sang themselves to birth . . . This and much more I read
in my books —.
Then all in a fever myself — I rushed out of the stifling house
— out of the city streets and on to the gorse golden hills. A
white road round the hills — there I walked — And below me

— like a beautiful Pre Raphaelite picture — lay the sea — and the violet mountains. The sky all a riot of rose and yellow — amethyst and purple —
At the foot of the hill — the city, but all curtained by a blue mist — that hung over it — in pale wreaths of Beauty.
No sound at all — and yet — the Silence — of that Prophetic Atmosphere — that is created by the Twilight only — I leaned against a low paling fence — in my brain thoughts were clashing with the sound of symbals — I felt Myself — by the power of my Youth — alone — God of it all —
Love and Fellowship — Work and Delicious Fascinating Pleasures — must exist for me — if I only search for them. Away out in the harbour lights shone from the ships — and now in the city too — golden beckoning flowers.

There came a sound of slowly moving horses — I saw coming towards me — a heavy carriage — slowly — slowly — coming towards me —
And I stood still — and waited.
The horses were hot and strained — the driver — muffled up to the eyes — it was very cold —
As it passed me — I saw — inside — an old man — his head fallen back among the cushions — the eyes closed — the mouth half open — and hands of Age crossed before him —
He was muttering to himself — mumbling, muttering.

Slowly it passed — and I watched it wind round the hill out of sight.

I turned again towards the sea and the mountains — the City and the golden lights — but Darkness had rushed across the sky.

Vignettes

I

Away beyond the line of dark houses there is a sound like the call of the sea after a storm — passionate, solemn, strong. I lean far out of my window in the warm, still night air. Down below, in the Mews, the little lamp is singing a silent song. It is the only glow of light in all this darkness. Men swilling the carriages with water; their sudden, sharp, exclamations; the faint, thin cry of a very young child, the chiming of a bell from the church close by — these are the only other sounds, impersonal, vague, intensely agitating.

It is at this hour and in this loneliness that London stretches out eager hands towards me, and in her eyes is the light of knowledge. 'In my streets,' she whispers, 'there is the passing of many feet, there are lines of flaring lights, there are cafes full of men and women, there is the intoxicating madness of night music, a great glamour of darkness, a tremendous anticipation, and, o'er all, the sound of laughter, half sad, half joyous, yet fearful, dying away in a strange shudder of satisfaction, and then swelling out into more laughter.' The men and women in the cafes hear it. They look at each other suddenly, swiftly, searchingly, and the lights seem stronger, the night music throbs yet more madly.

Out of the theatres a great crowd of people stream into the streets. There is the penetrating rhythm of the hansom cabs.

Convention has long since sought her bed. With blinds down, with curtains drawn, she is sleeping and dreaming.

Do you not *hear* the quick beat of my heart? Do you not *feel* the fierce rushing of blood through my veins?

In my streets there is the answer to all your achings and cryings. Prove yourself, permeate your senses with the heavy sweetness of the night. Let nothing remain hidden. Who knows that in the exploration of your mysteries you may find the answer to your questionings.

II

I lean out of my window. The dark houses stare at me and above them a great sweep of sky. Where it meets the houses there is a strange lightness — a suggestion, a promise.

Silence now in the Mews below. The cry of the child is silent, even the chiming of the bell is less frequent, no longer so persistent. But away beyond the line of the dark houses is a sound like the call of the sea after a storm. It is assuming gigantic proportions. Nearer and nearer it comes — a vast, incontrollable burst of sound.

And in its essence it is the faint, thin cry of the very young child. It is the old, old cry for the moon that rises eternally into the great vastness.

I lean from my window in the tower. Through the stillness comes the hushed sound of the fountain. I fancy I can hear the rose petals in the garden falling softly.

In the crude white moonlight a field of blue cabbages on my right shimmers like a cold sea. And before me, and round me, the beech woods rise, strong, black, and alluring. If I lean out far, and listen very intently, I hear a sound like the muttering of the darkness, the half-stifled breathing of the summer night. It is the heavy, indolent river slipping dreamily through the wide fields, and the luscious tangle of sweet rushes.

High among the beech woods stands the old castle, a mammoth skeleton, a vast, yawning, forsaken tomb, in whose grey shadows the sweet body of romance lies — long dead.

There is a light step in the garden below. It is Monsieur le Musician. Lantern in one hand, fiddle case in the other, he is strolling homeward from the cafe in the village. Riding through the village this evening I saw him seated at one of the green tables drinking much beer, and laughing loudly with Nicholas, the gardener, and Hans, the waiter.

Now he is a dream figure, stepping into the night picture with singular appropriateness of expression. I hear him softly whistling the opening bars of Max Bruch's D Minor Concerto. And a moment later he is gone.

A sudden faint breeze passes through the garden, and a wave of vague, agitating, bitter, sweet memories enwraps my heart in a darkness profound, inexplicable, silent.

III

Oh! this monotonous, terrible rain. The dull, steady, hopeless sound of it. I have drawn the curtains across the window to shut out the weeping face of the world — the trees swaying softly in their grief and dropping silver tears upon the brown earth, the narrow, sodden, mean, draggled wooden houses, colourless save for the dull, coarse red of the roof, and the long line of grey hills, impassable, spectral-like.

So I have drawn the curtains across my windows, and the light is intensely fascinating. A perpetual twilight broods here. The atmosphere is heavy with morbid charm. Strange, as I sit here, quiet, alone, how each possession of mine — the calendar gleaming whitely on the wall, each picture, each book, my 'cello case, the very furniture — seems to stir into life. The Velasquez Venus moves on her couch, ever so slightly; across the face of Manon a strange smile flickers for an instant, and is gone, my rocking chair is full of patient resignation, my 'cello case is wrapt in profound thought. Beside me a little bowl of mignonette is piercingly sweet, and a cluster of scarlet geraniums is hot with colour.

Sometimes through the measured sound of the rain comes the long, hopeless note of a foghorn far out at sea. And then all life seems but a crying out drearily, and a groping to and fro in a foolish, aimless darkness. Sometimes — it seems like miles away — I hear the sound of a door downstairs opening and shutting.

And I listen and think and dream until my life seems not *one* life, but a thousand million lives, and my soul is weighed down with the burden of past existence, with the vague, uneasy consciousness of future strivings.

And the grey thoughts fall upon my soul like the grey rain upon the world, but I cannot draw the curtain and shut it all out.

A year ago we sat by the fire, she and I, hand in hand, cheek to cheek, speaking but little, and then whispering, because the room was so dark, the fire so low, and the rain outside so loud and bitter.

She, a thin, little figure in a long, soft black frock, and a string of amethysts round her white throat.

Eventually it grew so cold that I dragged the blanket from the bed, and we wrapped ourselves up in it, smiling a little and saying, 'We feel like children on a desert island.' With one hand she held the rough, gaily-striped thing up to her chin; the other hand lay in mine. We talked of fame, how we both longed for it, how hard the struggle was, what we both meant to do. I found a piece of paper, and together we wrote a declaration vowing that in the space of one year we should have both become famous. And we signed the paper and sealed it; then, dedicating it to the gods, dropped it into the fire. For the moment a bright light, and then a handful of ashes. By and bye she fell softly asleep, and I gave her my share of the blanket, and arranged the sofa pillow in her low chair. The long night dragged coldly through, while I watched her, and thought, and longed, but could not sleep.

To-day, at the other end of the world, I have suffered, and she, doubtless, has bought herself a new hat at the February sales. *Sic transit gloria mundi.*

Silhouettes

It is evening, and very cold. From my window the laurestinus bush, in this half light, looks weighted with snow. It moves languidly, gently, backwards and forwards, and each time I look at it a delicate flower melody fills my brain.

Against the pearl sky the great hills tower, gorse-covered, leonine, magnificently savage. The air is quiet with still rain, yet, from the karaka tree comes a tremulous sound of bird song.

In the avenue three little boys are crouched under a tree smoking cigarettes. They are quite silent, and though terrified of discovery, their attitudes are full of luxurious abandon. . . . . And the grey smoke floats into the air — their incense, strong and perfumed, to the Great God of the Forbidden.

Two men pass down the avenue, talking eagerly. . . . In the house opposite are four beautiful squares of golden light. . . . My room is almost in darkness. The bed frightens me — it is so long and white. And the tassel of the window blind moves languidly to and fro. I cannot believe that it is not some living thing . . . .

It is growing very dark. The little boys, laughing shrilly, have left the avenue.

And I, leaning out of my window, alone, peering into the gloom, am seized by a passionate desire for everything that is hidden and forbidden. I want the night to come, and kiss me with her hot mouth, and lead me through an amethyst twilight to the place of the white gardenia . . . .

The laurestinus bush moves languidly, gently, backwards and forwards. There is a dull heavy sound of clocks striking far away, and, in my room, darkness, emptiness, save for the ghost-like bed. I feel to lie there quiet, silent, passively cold would be too fearful — yet — quite a little fascinating.

In the Botanical Gardens

They are such a subtle combination of the artificial and the natural — that is, partly, the secret of their charm.

From the entrance gate down the broad central walk, with the orthodox banality of carpet bedding on either side, stroll men and women and children — a great many children, who call to each other lustily, and jump up and down the green wooden seats. They seem as meaningless, as lacking in individuality, as the little figures in an impressionist landscape.

Above the carpet bedding, on one hand, there is a green hedge, and above the hedge a long row of cabbage trees. I stare up at them, and suddenly the green hedge is a stave, and the cabbage trees, now high, now low, have become an arrangement of notes — a curious, pattering, native melody.

In the enclosure the spring flowers are almost too beautiful — a great stretch of foam-like cowslips. As I bend over them, the air is heavy and sweet with their scent, like hay and new milk and the kisses of children, and, further on, a sunlit wonder of chiming daffodils.

Before me two great rhododendron bushes. Against the dark, broad leaves the blossoms rise, flame-like, tremulous in the still air, and the pearl rose loving-cup of a magnolia hangs delicately on the grey bough.

Everywhere there are clusters of china blue pansies, a mist of forget-me-nots, a tangle of anemones. Strange that these anemones — scarlet, and amethyst, and purple — vibrant with colour, always appear to me a trifle dangerous, sinister, seductive, but poisonous.

And, leaving the enclosure, I pass a little gully, filled with tree ferns, and lit with pale virgin lamps of arum lilies.

I turn from the smooth swept paths, and climb up a steep track, where the knotted tree roots have seared a rude pattern in the yellow clay. And suddenly, it disappears — all the pretty, carefully tended surface of gravel and sward and blossom, and there is bush, silent and splendid. On the green moss, on the brown earth, a wide splashing of yellow sunlight. And everywhere that strange indefinable scent. As I breathe it, it seems to absorb, to become part of me — and I am old with the age of centuries, strong with the strength of savagery.

Somewhere I hear the soft rhythmic flowing of water, and I follow the path down and down until I come to a little stream idly, dreamily floating past. I fling myself down, and put my hands in the water. An inexplicable, persistent feeling seizes me that I must become one with it all. Remembrance has gone — this is the Lotus Land — the green trees stir languorously, sleepily — there is the silver sound of a bird's call. Bending down, I drink a little of the water, Oh! is it magic? Shall I, looking intently, see vague forms lurking in the shadow staring at me malevolently, wildly, the thief of their birthright? Shall I, down the hillside, through the bush, ever in the shadow, see a great company moving towards me, their faces averted, wreathed with green garlands, passing, passing, following the little stream in silence until it is sucked into the wide sea . . . .

There is a sudden, restless movement, a pressure of the trees — they sway against one another — it is like the sound of weeping . . . .

I pass down the central walk towards the entrance gates. The men and women and children are crowding the pathway, looking reverently, admiringly, at the carpet bedding, spelling aloud the Latin names of the flowers.

Here is laughter and movement and bright sunlight — but behind me — is it near, or miles and miles away? — the bush lies hidden in the shadow.

Vignette — Westminster Cathedral

Did we ever climb that tower, Vere, you and I? Is it all a charming romance? . . .

Very languidly and dreamily we wandered through Westminster Cathedral. A faint, blue perfume of incense filled the air. In the chapel a woman was kneeling, the rosary falling — a little stream of silver through the ivory of her fingers.

Then we came to the heavily locked gates and stood before them, smiling at each other. An old man — I wonder if you remember his hands, they were rude, knotted, knarled hands — opened the gates and we passed through.

Looking back, those stairs seem to me to have been endless, an eternity of stone steps, then a great ascent of wooden ladders, and a narrow, dark staircase, twisting upwards. And sometimes, Vere, you were first, and sometimes I led the way. Often we rested, a little breathless, on a stone parapet, saying 'Can we go further?'

Always the thin blue perfume of the incense enveloped us. It filled the whole incident with dream atmosphere.

So, at last we reached the dome. A balcony had been built east and west, north and south — a little shrine to each of the four winds of Heaven. With a sensation of extraordinary relief, of lightness, we stepped out upon the balcony, and, below us, London was spread out like a charming, intricate tapestry . . . I think of it now, Vere, as a wonderful fusion of amethyst and silver.

And laughing, laughing childishly, with our hands on each other's shoulders, we watched the little people walking in the streets, like flies in the folds of some gigantic tablecloth.

The sky was filled with grey clouds . . . They floated by like a flock of silent birds. And I remember, far away the Crystal Palace shone, a monstrous pearl in an emerald setting.

We learned far over the parapet, and the four winds of Heaven seemed to beat upon us both. A long strand of your hair blew across my face, and the voice of London thundered out some stupendous, colossal, overwhelming fugue to the whole world — to us, clinging together outside the little tower.

'Do you think,' I said, 'in the evening when they have trimmed their lamps and set them in the blue dome of the sky, the ghosts may lean out, shoulder to shoulder, and point down to London and whisper "This is where I lived; in the Spring we walked there, together." Do you think, sometimes, sometimes, when there is no light in the sky-darkness, they have drowned their little flame in a passion of tears? . . '

'Look', you said, 'that is our street. Perhaps years hence, we shall look out and say — "In the third house, on the right-hand side, we kissed each other." '

Out of the wind, down the wooden ladders, down the stairs, we went together. The iron gate clanged to after us.

A service was being held in one of the chapels. While the people knelt, a great wave of music broke over, flooded the whole building. A boy in a long gown walked slowly up the aisle. He held in his arms a great spray of flowering lilies . . .

But you and I, Vere, passed out into the streets.

Vignette — Summer in Winter

Through the wild, Winter afternoon, Carlotta, at the piano, sang of Love.

Standing by the window, I watched her beautiful passionate profile. The walls were hung with daffodil silk. A faint golden light seemed to linger on her face. She wore a long black frock, and a hat with a drooping black feather. Her gloves, her great ermine coat, her silver purse were flung on the lounge beside her. The air was faintly scented with the perfume she loved that Winter — Peau d'Espagne.

There was a little fire of Juniper logs burning in the grate, the flames cast into the room strange, ghost-like shadows that leapt upon the curtains, upon the walls, that lurked behind the chairs and behind the lounge, that hid in the corners and seemed to point long shadow fingers at Carlotta.

She sang and sang, and the room seemed warm and full of sunshine and happy flowers. 'Come,' her voice cried to me, 'and we shall wander in a mystic garden filled with beautiful unexistent flowers. I alone possess the key. I alone can search out the secret paths. Lo there is a bower lit with the pale light of gardenia flowers . . . there are fountains filled with laughing water.'

I drew back the heavy curtain from the window. The rain was lashing against the glass. The house opposite appalled me — it was like the face of an old, old man drowned in tears. In the garden below rotting leaves were heaped upon the lawns and walks. The skeleton trees rattled together, and the wind had torn a rose bush from the ground. It sprawled across the path ugly and thorn-encrusted. Drearily, drearily fell the Winter rain upon the dead garden, upon the skeleton trees . . .

I turned from the window, and in the warm firelit room, with almost a note of defiance in her voice, Carlotta, at the piano, sang passionately of Love.

Leves Amores

I can never forget the Thistle Hotel. I can never forget that strange Winter night.

I had asked her to dine with me, and then go to the Opera. My room was opposite hers. She said she would come, but — could I do up her evening bodice, it was hooks at the back. Very well.

It was still daylight when I knocked at the door and entered. In her petticoat bodice and a full silk petticoat she was washing, sponging her face and neck. She said she was finished, and I might sit on the bed and wait for her. So I looked round at the dreary room. The one filthy window faced the street. She could see the choked, dust-grimed window of a wash-house opposite. For furniture, the room contained a low bed, draped with revolting, yellow, vine-patterned curtains, a chair, a wardrobe with a piece of cracked mirror attached, a washstand. But the wall paper hurt me physically. It hung in tattered strips from the wall. In its less discoloured and faded patches I could trace the pattern of roses — buds and flowers — and the frieze was a conventional design of birds, of what genus the good God alone knows.

And this was where she lived. I watched her curiously. She was pulling on long, thin stockings, and saying 'damn' when she could not find her suspenders. And I felt within me a certainty that nothing beautiful could ever happen in that room, and for her I felt, contempt, a little tolerance, a very little pity.

A dull, grey light hovered over everything; it seemed to accentuate the thin tawdriness of her clothes, the squalor of her life. She, too, looked dull and grey and tired. And I sat on the bed, and thought: 'Come, this Old Age. I have forgotten passion. I have been left behind in the beautiful golden procession of Youth. Now I am seeing life in the dressing-room of the theatre.'

So we dined somewhere and went to the Opera. It was late when we came out into the crowded night street, late and cold. She gathered up her long skirts. Silently we walked back to the Thistle Hotel, down the white pathway fringed with beautiful golden lilies, up the amethyst shadowed staircase.

Was Youth dead? . . . . *Was* Youth dead?

She told me as we walked along the corridor to her room that she was glad the night had come. I did not ask why. I was glad, too. It seemed a secret between us. So I went with her into her room to undo those troublesome hooks. She lit a little candle on an enamel bracket. The light filled the room with darkness. Like a sleepy child she slipped out of her frock, and then, suddenly, turned to me and flung her arms round my neck. Lo every bird upon the bulging frieze broke into song. Lo every rose upon the tattered paper budded and formed into blossom. Yes, even the green vine upon the bed curtains wreathed itself into strange chaplets and garlands, twined round us in a leafy embrace, held us with a thousand clinging tendrils.

And Youth was not dead.

In the Rangitaiki Valley

O valley of waving broom,
O lovely, lovely light,
O heart of the world, red-gold!
Breast high in the blossom I stand;
It beats about me like waves
Of a magical, golden sea.

The barren heart of the world
Alive at the kiss of the sun,
The yellow mantle of Summer
Flung over a laughing land,
Warm with the warmth of her body,
Sweet with the kiss of her breath.

O valley of waving broom,
O lovely, lovely light,
O mystical marriage of Earth
With the passionate Summer sun!
To her lover she holds a cup
And the yellow wine o'erflows.
He has lighted a little torch
And the whole of the world is ablaze.
Prodigal wealth of love!
Breast high in the blossom I stand.

Vignette — By the Sea

Lying thus on the sand, the foam washing over my hands, I am spellbound by the sea.

Behind the golden hills the sun is going down, a flaming jewel in a lurid setting, and there is a faint flush everywhere, on sea and land. To my right the sky has blossomed into a vivid rose, but, to my left, the land is hidden by a grey mist, lightened now here, now there, by the sun colour . . . It is like land seen from a ship, very far away, dreamland, mirage enchanted country.

Two sea birds, high in the air, fly screaming towards the light. It beats upon their white breasts, it flames upon their dull wings. Far away, a little boat is sailing upon the sweet water, a golden butterfly upon the dainty bosom of a mystic blossom . . .

And now the Italian fishermen are sailing in, their white sails bellying in the breeze. Several come rowing in a little boat. They spring ashore, the light shines upon their crisp, black hair, it shines on their faces, so that their skin is the colour of hot amber, on their bare legs and strong brown arms. They are dragging towards them the boat, the long, black, wet rope running through their fingers and falling in a bold pattern on the foam-blown sand . . . They call to one another — I cannot hear what they say — but against the long, rhythmic pulsing of the sea their voices sound curiously insignificant, like voices in a dream . . .

And there are exquisite golden-brown sprays and garlands of sea weed, set about with berries, white and brown. Are they flowers blown from the garden of the sea king's daughter? Does she wander through the delicate coral forests, seeking them, playing upon a little silver shell, her long hair floating behind her?

And near me there is a light upon the blue coast — steadily, tenderly it burns — a little candle set upon the great altar of the world.

The glow pales in the sky, on the land, but ever the long rhythmic pulsing of the sea. Oh, to sail and sail into the heart of the sea. Is it darkness and silence there, or is it a great light? . . .

So the grey sand slips, drifts through my fingers.

Night comes swiftly . . .

Study: The Death of a Rose

It is a sensation that can never be forgotten, to sit in solitude, in semi-darkness, and to watch the slow, sweet, shadowful death of a Rose.

Oh, to see the perfection of the perfumed petals being changed ever so slightly, as though a thin flame had kissed each with hot breath, and where the wounds bled the colour is savagely intense . . . I have before me such a Rose, in a thin, clear glass, and behind it a little spray of scarlet leaves. Yesterday it was beautiful with a certain serene, tearful, virginal beauty; it was strong and wholesome, and the scent was fresh and invigorating.

To-day it is heavy and languid with the loves of a thousand strange Things, who, lured by the gold of my candlelight, came in the Purple Hours, and kissed it hotly on the mouth, and sucked it into their beautiful lips with tearing, passionate desire.

. . . So now it dies . . . And I listen . . . for under each petal fold there lies the ghost of a dead melody, as frail and as full of suggestion as a ray of light upon a shadowed pool. Oh, divine sweet Rose. Oh, exotic and elusive and deliciously vague Death.

From the tedious sobbing and gasping, and hoarse guttural screaming, and uncouth repulsive movements of the body of dying Man, I draw apart, and, smiling, I lean over you, and watch your dainty, delicate Death.

Why Love is Blind

The Cupid child tired of the winter day
Wept and lamented for the skies of blue
Till, foolish child! he cried his eyes away —
And violets grew.

The Winter Fire

Winter without, but in the curtained room
Flushed into beauty by a fluttering fire
Shuttered and blinded from the ugly street
A woman sits — her hands locked round her knees
And bending forward . . . O'er her loosened hair
The firelight spins a web of shining gold
Sears her pale mouth with kisses passionate
Wraps her tired body in a hot embrace . .
Propped by the fender her rain sodden boots
Steam, and suspended from the iron bed
Her coat and skirt — her wilted, draggled hat.
But she is happy. Huddled by the fire
All recollections of the dim grey day
Dwindle to nothingness, and she forgets
That in the street outside the rain which falls
Muddies the pavement to a greasy brown.
That, in the morning she must start again
And search again for that which will not come —
She does not feel the sickening despair
That creeps into her bones throughout the day.
In her great eyes — dear Christ — the light of dreams
Lingered and shone. And she, a child again
Saw pictures in the fire. Those other days
The rambling house, the cool sweet scented rooms
The portraits on the walls, and China bowls
Filled with 'pot pourri'. On her rocking chair
Her sofa pillow broidered with her name —

19

She saw again her bedroom, very bare
The blue quilt worked with daisies white and gold
Where she slept, dreamlessly . . . .
. . . Opening her window, from the new mown lawn
The fragrant, fragrant scent of perfumed grass
The lilac tossing in the shining air
Its purple plumes. The laurustinus bush
Its blossoms like pale hands among the leaves
Quivered and swayed. And, Oh, the sun
That kisses her to life and warmth again
So she is young, and stretches out her arms . . . .
The woman, huddled by the fire, restlessly stirs
Sighing a little, like a sleepy child
While the red ashes crumble into grey . . . .

Suddenly, from the street, a burst of sound
A barrel organ, turned and jarred & wheezed
The drunken bestial, hiccoughing voice of London.

November

Dim mist of a fog-bound day . . .
From the lilac trees that droop in St Mary's Square
The dead leaves fall, a silent, shivering, cloud.
Through the grey haze the carts loom heavy, gigantic
Down the dull street. Children at play in the gutter
Quarrel and cry; their voices sound flat and toneless.
With a sound like the shuffling tread of some giant monster
I hear the trains escape from the stations near, and tear their
    way into the country.
Everything looks fantastic, repellent, I see from my window
An old man pass, dull, formless, like the stump of a dead tree
    moving.
The virginia creeper, like blood, streams down the face of the
    houses . . .
Even the railings, blackened and sharply defined, look evil and
    strangely malignant.
. . . Dim Mist of a fog-bound day,
From the lilac trees that droop in St Mary's Square
The dead leaves fall, a silent, fluttering crowd —
Dead leaves that shivering fall on the barren earth.
. . . Over and under it all, the muttering murmur of London.

Revelation

All through the Winter afternoon
We sat together, he and I . . . .
Down in the garden every tree
Seemed frozen to the sky

Yes, every twisted tree that bared
Its naked limbs for sacrifice
Was patterned like a monstrous weed
Upon a lake of ice.

It was as though the pallid world
Was gripped in the embrace of Death.
He wrapt the garden in his shroud
He killed it with his breath.

So through the Winter afternoon
We sat together by the fire
And in its heart, strange magic worlds
Would build, would flame, expire

In an intensity of flame —
Our books were heaped upon the floor
Fantastic chronicles of men
Of cities seen no more

Of countries buried by the sea
Of people who had laughed and cried
And madly suffered — who had held
The world — and then, had died —

A faded pageant of the past
Trooped by us in the gathering gloom
And we could hear strange, muffled cries
Like voices from the tomb.

And sometimes as we turned a page
We heard the shivering sound of rain
It trickled down the window glass
Like tears upon the pane.

We two, it seemed, were shut apart
Were fire bound from the Winter world
And all the secrets of the past
Lay like a scroll unfurled.

As through the winter afternoon
We dreaming, read of many lands
And woke . . . . to find the book of Life
Spread open in our hands.

The Trio

Out in the fog stained, mud stained street they stand
Two women and a man . . . Their draggled clothes
Hang on their withered bodies. It is cold
So cold the very rain and fog feel starved
And bite into their scarcely covered bones.
Their purple hands move restlessly, at first
They try to shield them with their thread-bare cuffs
Then thrust them in their coats, and then again
Blow on their fingers, but to no avail.
The women wear a strangely faded look
As though the rain which beat upon them both
And, never ceasing, always dripping down
Had worn away their features . . . In their eyes
Hunger had lit a pallid, wavering torch . . . .
The man is like a seedy, draggled bird
He frowns upon the women, savagely . . . . . .
Opposite them a warehouse, huge and grey
And ugly — in the ghostly light of fog
It looms gigantic — through the open doors

Men and more men are passing out and in.
. . . Then, at a signal from the draggled man
The women sing — God, from their withered mouths
A tragedy of singing issues forth
High pitched and wandering, crazy tuneless tunes
Over and over comes the same refrain
'Say, shepherds, have you seen my Flora pass this way.' . . . . .
The simple words hang trembling in the air
So strange, so foreign, if the filthy street
Had blossomed into daisies; if a vine
Had wreathed itself upon the warehouse wall
It would have been more natural — they sing
Shivering, starving — on their withered mouths
The winter day has set a frozen kiss . . . .
Coldly impassive, cynically grim
The warehouse seems to sneer at them and cry
'My doors are shut and bolted, locked and barred —
And in my bosom nurture I my spawn
Upon the blackened blood of my stone heart
I blind their eyes. I stop their mouths with dust
I hypnotise them with the chink of gold
They search and grope — but ever out of reach
I keep it, jingling. They can never bear
Your Floras and your shepherds . . .' Through the fog
The quavering voices fall and rise again . . .
Are silent — and the trio shuffles on.

Vignette — 'I look out through the window'

I look out through the window. A rhododendron bush sways restlessly, mysteriously, to and fro . . . The bare trees stand crucified against the opalescent sky.

In the next room someone is playing the piano. The sun shines whitely, touches the rhododendron leaves with soft color. (To and fro the branches sway, stretching upwards, outwards, so mysteriously; it is as though they moved in a dream. Through the open window, the cold air blowing in, stirs the heavy folds of the curtains . . . What is being played in the next room? . . . Does the music float through this room — and out of the window to the garden? Does the plant hear it, and answer to the sound? The music, too is strangely restless . . . it is seeking something . . . . perhaps this mystic, green plant, so faintly touched with colour . . . . .

. . . . . . I dream . . . And there is no plant, no music — only a restless, mysterious seeking a stretching upwards to the light — and outwards — a dream like movement.

What is it?

I look out into the garden at the bare trees crucified against the opalescent sky . . .

The sun is smothered under the white wing of a cloud — in the shadowed garden the plant is trembling.

Spring Wind in London

I blow across the stagnant world,
I blow across the sea,
For me, the sailor's flag unfurled,
For me, the uprooted tree.
My challenge to the world is hurled
The world must bow to me.

I drive the clouds across the sky,
I huddle them like sheep,
Merciless shepherd's dog am I
And shepherd's watch I keep.
If in the quiet vales they lie
I blow them up the steep.

Lo! In the treetops do I hide
In every living thing
On the moon's yellow wings I glide
On the wild rose I swing
On the sea horse's back I ride
And what then do I bring?

And when a little child is ill
I pause, and with my hand
I wave the window curtain's frill
That he may understand
Outside the wind is blowing still
. . . It is a pleasant land.

Oh, stranger in a foreign place
See what I bring to you,
This rain — is tears upon your face
I tell you — tell you true
I came from that forgotten place
Where once the wattle grew.

All the wild sweetness of the flower
Tangled against the wall
It was that magic, silent hour . . . .
The branches grew so tall
They twined themselves into a bower
The sun shone . . . . and the fall

Of yellow blossom on the grass!
You feel that golden rain
Both of you could not hold, alas,
Both of you tried — in vain.
A memory, stranger. So I pass . . . .
It will not come again.

The Arabian Shawl

'It is cold outside, you will need a coat —
What! this old Arabian shawl!
Bind it about your head and throat,
These steps . . . it is dark . . . my hand . . . you might fall.'

What has happened? What strange, sweet charm
Lingers about the Arabian shawl . . .
Do not tremble so! There can be no harm
In just remembering — that is all.

'I love you so — I will be your wife,'
Here, in the dark of the Terrace wall,
Say it again. Let that other life
Fold us like the Arabian shawl.

'Do you remember?' . . . 'I quite forget,
Some childish foolishness, that is all,
To-night is the first time we have met . . .
Let me take off my Arabian shawl!'

Sleeping Together

Sleeping together . . . how tired you were! . . .
How warm our room . . . how the firelight spread
On walls and ceiling and great white bed!
We spoke in whispers as children do,
And now it was I — and then it was you
Slept a moment, to wake — 'My dear,
I'm not at all sleepy,' one of us said . . . .

Was it a thousand years ago?
I woke in your arms — you were sound asleep —
And heard the pattering sound of sheep.
Softly I slipped to the floor and crept
To the curtained window, then, while you slept,
I watched the sheep pass by in the snow.

O flock of thoughts with their shepherd Fear
Shivering, desolate, out in the cold,
That entered into my heart to fold!
A thousand years . . . was it yesterday
When we, two children of far away,
Clinging close in the darkness, lay
Sleeping together? . . . How tired you were! . . .

The Quarrel

Our quarrel seemed a giant thing,
It made the room feel mean and small,
The books, the lamp, the furniture,
The very pictures on the wall —

Crowded upon us as we sat
Pale and terrified, face to face.
'Why do you stay?' she said, 'my room
Can never be your resting place.'

'Katinka, ere we part for life,
I pray you walk once more with me.'
So down the dark, familiar road
We paced together, silently.

The sky — it seemed on fire with stars!
I said: — 'Katinka dear, look up!'
Like thirsty children, both of us
Drank from that giant loving cup.

'Who were those *dolls*?' Katinka said.
'What were their stupid, vague alarms?'
And suddenly we turned and laughed
And rushed into each other's arms.

To Stanislaw Wyspianski

From the other side of the world,
From a little island cradled in the giant sea bosom,
From a little land with no history,
(Making its own history, slowly and clumsily
Piecing together this and that, finding the pattern, solving
    the problem,
Like a child with a box of bricks),
I, a woman, with the taint of the pioneer in my blood,
Full of a youthful strength that wars with itself and is lawless,
I sing your praises, magnificent warrior; I proclaim your
    triumphant battle.
My people have had nought to contend with;
They have worked in the broad light of day and handled the
    clay with rude fingers
Life — a thing of blood and muscle; Death — a shovelling
    underground of waste material.
What would they know of ghosts and unseen presences,
Of shadows that blot out reality, of darkness that stultifies
    morn?
Fine and sweet the water that runs from their mountains;
How could they know of poisonous weed, of rotted and
    clogging tendrils?
And the tapestry woven from dreams of your tragic childhood
They would tear in their stupid hands,
The sad, pale light of your soul blow out with their childish
    laughter.
But the dead — the old — Oh Master, we belong to you there;
Oh Master, there we are children and awed by the strength of a
    giant;
How alive you leapt into the grave and wrestled with Death
And found in the veins of Death the red blood flowing
And raised Death up in your arms and showed him to all the
    people.
Yours a more personal labor than the Nazarene's miracles,

Yours a more forceful encounter than the Nazarene's gentle
    commands.
Stanislaw Wyspianski — Oh man with the name of a fighter,
Across these thousands of sea-shattered miles we cry and
    proclaim you;
We say 'He is lying in Poland, and Poland thinks he is dead;
But he gave the denial to Death — he is lying there, wakeful;
The blood in his giant heart pulls red through his veins.'

Loneliness

Now it is Loneliness who comes at night
Instead of Sleep, to sit beside my bed.
Like a tired child I lie and wait her tread,
I watch her softly blowing out the light.
Motionless sitting, neither left nor right
She turns, and weary, weary droops her head.
She, too, is old; she, too, has fought the fight.
So, with the laurel she is garlanded.

Through the sad dark the slowly ebbing tide
Breaks on a barren shore, unsatisfied.
A strange wind flows . . . then silence. I am fain
To turn to Loneliness, to take her hand,
Cling to her, waiting, till the barren land
Fills with the dreadful monotone of rain.

The Sea Child

Into the world you sent her, mother,
  Fashioned her body of coral and foam,
Combed a wave in her hair's warm smother,
  And drove her away from home.

In the dark of the night she crept to the town
  And under a doorway she laid her down,
The little blue child in the foam-fringed gown.

And never a sister and never a brother
  To hear her call, to answer her cry.
Her face shone out from her hair's warm smother
  Like a moonkin up in the sky.

She sold her corals; she sold her foam;
  Her rainbow heart like a singing shell
Broke in her body: she crept back home.

Peace, go back to the world, my daughter,
  Daughter, go back to the darkling land;
There is nothing here but sad sea water,
  And a handful of sifting sand.

The Opal Dream Cave

In an opal dream cave I found a fairy:
Her wings were frailer than flower petals —
Frailer far than snowflakes.
She was not frightened, but poised on my finger,
Then delicately walked into my hand.
I shut the two palms of my hands together
And held her prisoner.
I carried her out of the opal cave,
Then opened my hands.
First she became thistledown,
Then a mote in a sunbeam,
Then — nothing at all.
Empty now is my opal dream cave.

Sea

The Sea called — lay on the rocks and said:
'I am come.'
She mocked and showed her teeth,
Stretching out her long green arms.
'Go away!' she thundered.
'Then tell me what I am to do,' I begged.
'If I leave you, you will not be silent,
But cry my name in the cities
And wistfully entreat me in the plains and forests;
All else I forsake to come to you — what must I do?'
'Never have I uttered your name,' snarled the Sea.
'There is no more of me in your body
Than the little salt tears you are frightened of shedding.
What can you know of my love on your brown rock
    pillow . . . .
Come closer.'

Along the Gray's Inn Road

Over an opaque sky grey clouds moving heavily like the wings of tired birds. Wind blowing: in the naked light buildings and people appear suddenly grotesque — too sharply modelled, maliciously tweaked into being.

A little procession wending its way up the Gray's Inn Road. In front, a man between the shafts of a hand-barrow that creaks under the weight of a piano-organ and two bundles. The man is small and greenish brown, head lolling forward, face covered with sweat. The piano-organ is bright red, with a blue and gold 'dancing picture' on either side. The big bundle is a woman. You see only a black mackintosh topped with a sailor hat; the little bundle she holds has chalk-white legs and yellow boots dangling from the loose ends of the shawl. Followed by two small boys, who walk with short steps, staring intensely at the ground, as though afraid of stumbling over their feet.

No word is spoken; they never raise their eyes. And this silence and pre-occupation gives to their progress a strange dignity.

They are like pilgrims straining forward to Nowhere, dragging, and holding to, and following after that bright red, triumphant thing with the blue and gold 'dancing picture' on either side.

The Secret

In the profoundest Ocean
There is a rainbow shell,
It is always there, shining most stilly
Under the greatest storm waves
And under the happy little waves
That the old Greek called 'ripples of laughter.'
And you listen, the rainbow shell
Sings in the profoundest ocean —
It is always there, singing most silently . . !

Very Early Spring

The fields are snowbound no longer
There are little blue lakes and flags of tenderest green.
The snow has been caught up into the sky
So many white clouds — and the blue of the sky is cold.
Now the sun walks in the forest
He touches the boughs and stems with his golden fingers
They shiver, and wake from slumber.
Over the barren branches he shakes his yellow curls.
. . . . Yet is the forest full of the sound of tears . . . .
A wind dances over the fields.
Shrill and clear the sound of her waking laughter,
Yet the little blue lakes tremble
And the flags of tenderest green bend and quiver.

The Awakening River

The gulls are mad-in-love with the river
And the river unveils her face and smiles.
In her sleep-brooding eyes they mirror their shining wings.
She lies on silver pillows: the sun leans over her.
He warms and warms her, he kisses and kisses her.
There are sparks in her hair and she stirs in laughter.
Be careful, my beautiful waking one! you will catch on fire.
Wheeling and flying with the foam of the sea on their breasts
The ineffable mists of the sea clinging to their wild wings
Crying the rapture of the boundless ocean.
The gulls are mad-in-love with the river.
Wake! we are the dream thoughts flying from your heart.
Wake! we are the songs of desire flowing from your bosom.
O, I think the sun will lend her his great wings
And the river will fly away to the sea with the mad-in-love
    birds.

The Earth-Child in the Grass

In the very early morning
Long before Dawn time
I lay down in the paddock
And listened to the cold song of the grass.
Between my fingers the green blades,
And the green blades pressed against my body.
'Who is she leaning so heavily upon me?'
Sang the grass.
'Why does she weep on my bosom,
Mingling her tears with the tears of my mystic lover?
Foolish little earth child!
It is not yet time.
One day I shall open my bosom
And you shall slip in — but not weeping.
Then in the early morning
Long before Dawn time
Your lover will lie in the paddock.
Between his fingers the green blades
And the green blades pressed against his body . . .
My song shall not sound cold to him
In my deep wave he will find the wave of your hair
In my strong sweet perfume, the perfume of your kisses.
Long and long he will lie there . . .
Laughing — not weeping.'

To God the Father

To the little, pitiful God I make my prayer,
The God with the long grey beard
And flowing robe fastened with a hempen girdle
Who sits nodding and muttering on the all-too-big throne of
Heaven.
What a long, long time, dear God, since you set the stars in
their places,
Girded the earth with the sea, and invented the day and night.
And longer the time since you looked through the blue window
of Heaven
To see your children at play in a garden . . . .
Now we are all stronger than you and wiser and more
arrogant,
In swift procession we pass you by.
'Who is that marionette nodding and muttering
On the all-too-big throne of Heaven?
Come down from your place, Grey Beard,
We have had enough of your play-acting!'
It is centuries since I believed in you,
But to-day my need of you has come back.
I want no rose-coloured future,
No books of learning, no protestations and denials —
I am sick of this ugly scramble,
I am tired of being pulled about —
O God, I want to sit on your knees
On the all-too-big throne of Heaven,
And fall asleep with my hands tangled in your grey beard.

Floryan nachdenklich

Floryan sits in the black chintz chair,
An Indian curtain behind his head
Blue and brown and white and red.
Floryan sits quite still — quite still.
There is a noise like a rising tide
Of wind and rain in the black outside.
But the firelight leaps on Floryan's wall
And the Indian curtain suddenly seems
To stir and shake with a thousand dreams.
The Indian flowers drink the fire
As though it were sun, and the Indian leaves
Patter and sway to an echo breeze.
On the great brown boughs of the Indian tree
Little birds sing and preen their wings.
They flash through the sun like jewel rings.
And the great tree grows and moves and spreads
Through the silent room, and the rising tide
Of wind and rain on the black outside
Fades — and Floryan suddenly stirs
And lifts his eyes and weeps to see
The dreaming flowers of the Indian tree.

Jangling Memory

Heavens above! here's an old tie of yours —
Sea-green dragons stamped on a golden ground.
Ha! Ha! Ha! What children we were in those days.

Do you love me enough to wear it now —
Have you the courage of your pristine glories?
Ha! Ha! Ha! You laugh and shrug your shoulders.

Those were the days when a new tie spelt a fortune:
We wore it in turn — I flaunted it as a waist-belt.
Ha! Ha! Ha! What easily satisfied babies.

I think I'll turn it into a piano duster.
'Give it to me, I'll polish my slippers on it!'
Ha! Ha! Ha! The rag's not worth the dustbin.

'Throw the shabby old thing right out of the window;
Fling it into the faces of other children!'
Ha! Ha! Ha! We laughed and laughed till the tears came!

There was a Child Once

There was a child once.
He came to play in my garden;
He was quite pale and silent.
Only when he smiled I knew everything about him,
I knew what he had in his pockets,
And I knew the feel of his hands in my hands
And the most intimate tones of his voice.
I led him down each secret path,
Showing him the hiding-place of all my treasures.
I let him play with them, every one,
I put my singing thoughts in a little silver cage
And gave them to him to keep . . . .
It was very dark in the garden
But never dark enough for us. On tiptoe we walked among the
      deepest shades;
We bathed in the shadow pools beneath the trees,
Pretending we were under the sea.
Once — near the boundary of the garden —
We heard steps passing along the World-road;
Oh, how frightened we were!
I whispered: 'Have you ever walked along that road?'
He nodded, and we shook the tears from our eyes . . . .
There was a child once.
He came — quite alone — to play in my garden;
He was pale and silent.
When we met we kissed each other,
But when he went away, we did not even wave.

Sea Song

I will think no more of the sea!
Of the big green waves
And the hollowed shore,
Of the brown rock caves
No more, no more
Of the swell and the weed
And the bubbling foam.

Memory dwells in my far away home,
She has nothing to do with me.

She is old and bent
With a pack
On her back.
Her tears all spent,
Her voice, just a crack.
With an old thorn stick
She hobbles along,
And a crazy song
Now slow, now quick
Wheeks in her throat.

And every day
While there's light on the shore
She searches for something
Her withered claw
Tumbles the seaweed;
She pokes in each shell
Groping and mumbling
Until the night
Deepens and darkens,
And covers her quite,
And bids her be silent,
And bids her be still.

The ghostly feet
Of the whispery waves
Tiptoe beside her.
They follow, follow
To the rocky caves
In the white beach hollow . . .
She hugs her hands,
She sobs, she shrills,
And the echoes shriek
In the rocky hills.
She moans: it is lost!
Let it be! Let it be!
I am old. I'm too cold
I am frightened . . . the sea
Is too loud . . . it is lost,
It is gone . . . Memory
Wails in my far away home.

The Meeting

We started speaking —
Looked at each other; then turned away —
The tears kept rising to my eyes
But I could not weep
I wanted to take your hand
But my hand trembled.
You kept counting the days
Before we should meet again
But both of us felt in our heart
That we parted for ever and ever.
The ticking of the little clock filled the quiet room —
Listen I said; it is so loud
Like a horse galloping on a lonely road.
As loud as that — a horse galloping past in the night.
You shut me up in your arms —
But the sound of the clock stifled our hearts' beating.

You said 'I cannot go: all that is living of me
Is here for ever and ever.'
Then you went.
The world changed. The sound of the clock grew fainter
Dwindled away — became a minute thing —
I whispered in the darkness: 'If it stops, I shall die.'

Countrywomen

These be two
Country women
What a size!
Grand big arms
And round red faces
Big substantial
Sit down places
Great big bosoms
Firm as cheese
Bursting through their country jacket
Wide big laps
And sturdy knees
Hands out spread
Round and rosy
Hands to hold
A country posy
Or a baby or a lamb
And such eyes!
Stupid, shifty, small and sly
Peeping through a slit of sty
Squinting through a neighbour's placket.

Stars

Most merciful God
Look kindly upon
An impudent child
Who wants sitting on.
This evening late
I went to the door
And then to the gate
There were more stars — more
Than I could have expected
Even I!
I was simply amazed
Almighty, August.
I was utterly dazed,
Omnipotent, Just
In a word I was floored
Good God of Hosts — Lord!
That at this time of day
They should still blaze away
That Thou hadst not rejected
Or at least circumspected
Their white silver beauty
. . Was it spite . . Was it duty . . ?

Deaf House Agent

That deaf old man
With his hand to his ear —
His hand to his head stood out like a shell,
Horny and hollow. He said, 'I can't hear.'
He muttered, 'Don't shout,
I can hear very well!'
He mumbled, 'I can't catch a word;
I can't follow.'
Then Jack with a voice like a Protestant bell
Roared — 'Particulars! Farmhouse! At ten quid a year!'
'I dunno wot place you are talking about,'
Said the deaf old man.
Said Jack, 'What the HELL!'

   But the deaf old man took a pin from his
      desk, picked a piece of wool the size of
      a hen's egg from his ear, had a good look
      at it, decided in its favour and replaced
      it in the aforementioned organ.

Villa Pauline

But Ah! before he came
You were only a name
Four little rooms and cupboard
Without a bone,
And I was alone!
Now with your windows wide
Everything from outside
Of sun and flower and loveliness
Comes in to hide —
To play to laugh on the stairs
To catch unawares
Our childish happiness
And to glide
Through the four little rooms on tip toe
With lifted finger,
Pretending we shall not know
When the shutters are shut
That they still linger
Long long after
Lying close in the dark
He says to me hark,
Isn't that laughter?

Camomile Tea

Outside the sky is light with stars
There's a hollow roaring from the sea
And alas for the little almond flowers!
The wind is shaking the almond tree.

How little I thought a year ago
In that horrible cottage upon the Lee
That Bogey and I should be sitting so
And sipping a cup of camomile tea.

Light as feathers the witches fly
The horn of the moon is plain to see.
By a firefly under a jonquil flower
A goblin is toasting a bumble-bee.

We might be fifty we might be five
So snug so compact so wise are we!
Under the kitchen table leg
My knee is pressing against Jack's knee.

But our shutters are shut the fire is low
The tap is dripping peacefully
The saucepan shadows on the wall
Are black and round and plain to see.

Waves

I saw a tiny God
Sitting
Under a bright blue Umbrella
That had white tassels
And forked ribs of gold
Below him His little world
Lay open to the sun
The shadow of his Hat
Lay upon a city
When he stretched forth His hand
A lake became a dark tremble
When he kicked up his foot
It became night in the mountain passes.

But thou art small!
There are gods far greater than thee
They rise and fall
The tumbling gods of the sea.
Can thy Breast heave such sighs
Such hollow savage cries
Such windy breath
Such groaning death
And can thy arm enfold
The old the cold
The changeless dreadful places
Where the herds
Of horned sea monsters
And the screaming birds
Gather together.
From those silent men
That lie in the pen
Of our pearly prisons —
Canst thou hunt thy prey
Like us canst thou stay

Awaiting thine hour
And then rise like a tower
And crash and shatter?

There are neither trees nor bushes
In my country
Said the Tiny God
But there are streams
And waterfalls
And mountain peaks
Covered with lovely weed
There are little shores and safe harbours
Caves for cool, and plains for sun and wind.
Lovely is the sound of the rivers
Lovely the flashing brightness
Of the lovely peaks.
I am content.

But thy kingdom is small
Said the God of the Sea —
Thy kingdom shall fall
I shall not let thee be.
Thou art proud.
With a loud
Pealing of laughter
He rose and covered
The tiny god's land
With the tip of his hand
With the curl of his fingers
And after . . .

The Tiny God
Began to cry —

The Town Between the Hills

The further the little girl leaped and ran
The further she longed to be
The white white fields of jonquil flowers
Danced up as high as her knee
And flashed and sparkled before her eyes
Until she could hardly see
So to the wood went she.

It was quiet in the wood
It was solemn and grave
A sound like a wave
Sighed in the tree tops
And then sighed no more
But she was brave
And the sky showed through
A bird egg's blue
And she saw
A tiny path that was running away
Over the hills to who can say —
She ran too.
But then the path broke
Then the path ended
And wouldn't be mended.
A little old man
Sat on the edge
Hugging the hedge
He had a fire
And 2 eggs in a pan —
And a paper poke
Of pepper and salt
So she came to a halt
To watch and admire
Cunning and nimble was he!
May I help if I can little old man?

50

Bravo he said
You can dine with me
I've two old eggs
From 2 white hens
And a loaf from a kind ladie
Some fresh nutmegs
Some cutlet ends
In pink and white paper frills
And — I've — got
A little hot pot
From the town between the Hills.
He nodded his head
And made her a sign
To sit under the spray
Of a trailing vine.
But when the little girl joined her hands
And said the grace she had learned to say
The little old man gave 2 dreadful squeals
And she just saw the flash of his smoking heels
As he tumbled tumbled
With his two old eggs
From 2 white hens
His loaf from a kind ladie
The fresh nutmegs
The cutlet-ends
In the pink and white paper frills
And away rumbled
Little hot-pot so much too hot
From the town between the hills.

Voices of the air!

But then there comes that moment rare
When for no cause that I can find
The little voices of the air
Sound above all the sea and wind.

The sea and wind do then obey.
And sighing sighing double notes
Of double basses, content to play
A droning chord for the little throats.

The little throats that sing and rise
Up into the light with lovely ease
And a kind of magical sweet surprise
To hear and to know themselves for these —

For these little voices: the bee, the fly
The leaf that taps — the pod that breaks —
The breeze on the grass-tops bending by —
The shrill quick sound that the insect makes —

Sanary

Her little hot room looked over the bay
Through a stiff palisade of glinting palms
And there she would lie in the heat of the day
Her dark head resting upon her arms
So quiet so still she did not seem
To think to feel or even to dream.

The shimmering blinding web of sea
Hung from the sky and the spider sun
With busy frightening cruelty
Crawled over the sky and spun and spun
She could see it still when she shut her eyes
And the little boats caught in the web like flies.

Down below at this idle hour
Nobody walked in the dusty street
A scent of dying mimosa flower
Lay on the air but sweet — too sweet.

To L. H. B. (1894-1915)

Last night for the first time since you were dead
I walked with you, my brother, in a dream.
We were at home again beside the stream
Fringed with tall berry bushes, white and red.
'Don't touch them: they are poisonous,' I said.
But your hand hovered, and I saw a beam
Of strange bright laughter flying round your head
And as you stooped I saw the berries gleam —
'Don't you remember? We called them Dead Man's Bread!'
I woke and heard the wind moan and the roar
Of the dark water tumbling on the shore.
Where — where is the path of my dream for my eager feet?
By the remembered stream my brother stands
Waiting for me with berries in his hands . . .
'These are my body. Sister, take and eat.'

Butterflies

In the middle of our porridge plates
There was a blue butterfly painted
And each morning we tried who should reach the butterfly
    first.
Then the Grandmother said: 'Do not eat the poor butterfly.'
That made us laugh.
Always she said it and always it started us laughing.
It seemed such a sweet little joke.
I was certain that one fine morning
The butterflies would fly out of the plates
Laughing the teeniest laugh in the world
And perch on the Grandmother's cap.

The Candle

By my bed, on a little, round table
The Grandmother placed a candle
She gave me three kisses telling me they were three dreams
And tucked me in just where I loved being tucked.
Then she went out of the room and the door was shut.
I lay still, waiting for my three dreams to talk
But they were silent.
Suddenly I remembered giving her three kisses back
Perhaps, by mistake, I had given my three little dreams.
I sat up in bed.
The room grew — big, O bigger far than a church.
The wardrobe, quite by itself, as big as a house
And the jug on the washstand smiled at me . . .
It was not a friendly smile.
I looked at the basket chair where my clothes lay folded
The chair gave a creak as though it were listening for
        something
Perhaps it was coming alive and going to dress in my clothes.
But the awful thing was the window
I could not think what was outside —
No tree to be seen, I was sure,
No nice little plant or friendly pebbly path.
Why did she pull down the blind every night?
It was better to know.
I crunched my teeth and crept out of bed
I peeped through a slit of the blind
There was nothing at all to be seen
But hundreds of friendly candles all over the sky
In remembrance of frightened children.
I went back to bed . . .
The three dreams started singing a little song.

The Grandmother

Underneath the cherry trees
The Grandmother in her lilac printed gown
Carried Little Brother in her arms.
A wind, no older than Little Brother
Shook the branches of the cherry trees
So that the blossom snowed on her hair
And on her faded lilac gown.
I said: 'May I see?'
She bent down and lifted a corner of his shawl.
He was fast asleep.
But his mouth moved as if he were kissing.
'Beautiful,' said Grandmother, nodding and smiling.
But my lips quivered.
And looking at her kind face
I wanted to be in the place of Little Brother
To put my arms round her neck
And kiss the two tears that shone in her eyes.

Little Brother's Secret

When my birthday was coming
Little Brother had a secret
He kept it for days and days
And just hummed a little tune when I asked him.
But one night it rained
And I woke up and heard him crying.
Then he told me.
'I planted two lumps of sugar in your garden
Because you love it so frightfully
I thought there would be a whole sugar tree for your birthday
And now it will all be melted.'
O, the darling!

Little Brother's Story

We sat in front of the fire
Grandmother was in the rocking chair doing her knitting
And Little Brother and I were lying down flat.
'Please tell us a story, Grandmother,' we said
But she put her head on one side and began counting the
      stitches
'Suppose you tell me one instead.'
I made up one about a spotted tiger
That had a knot in his tail
But though *I* liked that about the knot
I did not know why it was put there
So I said: 'Little Brother's turn.'
'I know a perfect story,' he cried, waving his hands.
Grandmother laid down her knitting.
'Do tell us, dear.'
'Once upon a time there was a bad little girl
And her Mummy gave her the slipper — and that's all.'
It was not a very special story.
But we pretended to be very pleased —
And Grandmother gave him jumps on her lap.

The Man with the Wooden Leg

There was a man lived quite near us
He had a wooden leg and a goldfinch in a green cage
His name was Farkey Anderson
And he'd been in a war to get his leg.
We were very sad about him
Because he had such a beautiful smile
And was such a big man to live in a very little house.
When he walked on the road his leg did not matter so much
But when he walked in his little house
It made an ugly noise.
Little Brother said his goldfinch sang the loudest of all other
    birds
So that he should not hear his poor leg
And feel too sorry about it.

When I was a Bird

I climbed up the karaka tree
Into a nest all made of leaves
But soft as feathers
I made up a song that went on singing all by itself
And hadn't any words but got sad at the end.
There were daisies in the grass under the tree.
I said, just to try them:
'I'll bite off your heads and give them to my little children to
    eat.'
But they didn't believe I was a bird
They stayed quite open.
The sky was like a blue nest with white feathers
And the sun was the mother bird keeping it warm.
That's what my song said: though it hadn't any words.
Little Brother came up the path, wheeling his barrow
I made my dress into wings and kept very quiet
Then when he was quite near I said: 'sweet — sweet.'
For a moment he looked quite startled —
Then he said: 'Pooh, you're not a bird; I can see your legs.'
But the daisies didn't really matter
And Little Brother didn't really matter —
I felt *just* like a bird.

The Gulf

A gulf of silence separates us from each other
I stand at one side of the gulf — you at the other
I cannot see you or hear you — yet know that you are there —
Often I call you by your childish name
And pretend that the echo to my crying is your voice.
How can we bridge the gulf — never by speech or touch
Once I thought we might fill it quite up with our tears
Now I want to shatter it with our laughter.

The Storm

I ran to the forest for shelter
Breathless, half sobbing
I put my arms round a tree
Pillowed my head against the rough bark
Protect me, I said. I am a lost child.
But the tree showered silver drops on my face and hair.
A wind sprang up from the ends of the earth
It lashed the forest together
A huge green wave burst and thundered over my head.
I prayed, implored, 'Please take care of me.'
But the wind pulled at my cloak and the rain beat upon me.
Little rivers tore up the ground and swamped the bushes.
A frenzy possessed the earth: I felt that the earth was drowning
In a bubbling cavern of space. I alone —
Smaller than the smallest fly — was alive and terrified.
Then, for what reason I know not, I became triumphant.
Well kill me — I cried — and ran out into the open.
But the storm ceased: the sun spread his wings
And floated serene in the silver pool of the sky.
I put my hands over my face: I was blushing
And the trees swung together and delicately laughed.

Across the Red Sky

Across the red sky two birds flying
Flying with drooping wings
Silent and solitary their ominous flight.
All day the triumphant sun with yellow banners
Warred and warred with the earth and when she yielded
Stabbed her heart gathered her blood in a chalice
Spilling it over the evening sky.
When the dark plumaged birds go flying flying
Quiet lies the earth wrapt in her mournful shadow
Her sightless eyes turned to the red sky
And the restlessly seeking birds.

Night Scented Stock

White, white in the milky night
The moon danced over a tree
'Wouldn't it be lovely to swim in the lake!'
Someone whispered to me.

'Oh, do–do–do!' cooed someone else
And clasped her hands to her chin.
'I should so love to see the white bodies
All the white bodies jump in!'

The big dark house hid secretly
Behind the magnolia and the spreading pear tree
But there was a sound of music — music rippled and ran
Like a lady laughing behind her fan
Laughing and mocking and running away —
Come into the garden — it's as light as day!

'I can't dance to that Hungarian stuff
The rhythm in it is not passionate enough'
Said somebody. 'I absolutely refuse . .'
But he took off his socks and his shoes
And round he spun. 'It's like Hungarian fruit dishes
Hard and bright — a mechanical blue!'
His white feet flicked in the grass like fishes . .
Some one cried: 'I want to dance, too!'

But one with a queer russian ballet head
Curled up on a blue wooden bench instead.
And another, shadowy — shadowy and tall
Walked in the shadow of the dark house wall,
Someone beside her. It shone in the gloom,
His round grey hat like a wet mushroom.

'Don't you think, perhaps . .' piped someone's flute . .
'How sweet the flowers smell!' I heard the other say —
Somebody picked a wet, wet pink
Smelled it and threw it away.

'Is the moon a virgin or is she a harlot?'
Asked somebody. Nobody would tell.
The faces and the hands moved in a pattern
As the music rose and fell.

In a dancing, mysterious, moon bright pattern
Like flowers nodding under the sea
The music stopped and there was nothing left of them
But the moon dancing over the tree.

Now I am a Plant, a Weed

Now I am a plant, a weed
Bending and swinging
On a rocky ledge
And now I am long brown grass
Fluttering like flame
I am a reed
An old shell singing
For ever the same
A drift of sedge
A white, white stone
A bone
Until I pass
Into sand again
And spin and blow
To and fro, to and fro
On the edge of the sea
In the fading light . .
    For the light fades.

But if you were to come you would not say
She is not waiting here for me
She has forgotten. Have we not in play
Disguised ourselves as weed and stones and grass
While the strange ships did pass
Gently — gravely — leaving a curl of foam
That uncurled softly about our island home
Bubbles of foam that glittered on the stone
Like rainbows. Look darling! No, they are gone.
And the white sails have melted into the sailing sky . .

There is a Solemn Wind To-Night

There is a solemn wind to-night
   That sings of solemn rain;
The trees that have been quiet so long
   Flutter and start again.

The slender trees, the heavy trees,
   The fruit trees laden and proud,
Lift up their branches to the wind
   That cries to them so loud.

The little bushes and the plants
   Bow to the solemn sound,
And every tiniest blade of grass
   Shakes on the quiet ground.

Out in the Garden

Out in the garden
Out in the windy, swinging dark
Under the trees and over the flower beds
Over the grass and under the hedge border
Someone is sweeping sweeping
Some old gardener
Out in the windy swinging dark
Someone is secretly putting in order
Someone is creeping creeping.

Strawberries and the Sailing Ship

We sat on the top of the cliff
Overlooking the open sea
Our backs turned to the little town
Each of us had a basket of strawberries
We had just bought them from a dark woman
With quick eyes — berry-finding eyes
They're fresh picked said she from our own garden
The tips of her fingers were stained a bright red!
Heavens what strawberries
Each one was the finest
The perfect berry — the strawberry Absolute
The fruit of our childhood!
The very air came fanning
On strawberry wings
And down below, in the pools
Little children were bathing
With strawberry faces.
Over the blue swinging water
A three masted sailing ship
With nine ten eleven sails
Wonderfully beautifully!
She came riding
As though every sail were taking its fill
of the sun and the light.
And Oh! how I'd love to be on board said Anne.
The captain was below, but the crew lay about
Idle and handsome —
Have some strawberries we said
Slipping and sliding on the polished decks
And shaking the baskets.

Malade

The man in the room next to mine
Has got the same complaint as I
When I wake in the night I hear him turning
And then he coughs
And I cough
And he coughs again —
This goes on for a long time —
Until I feel we are like two roosters
Calling to each other at false dawn
From far away hidden farms

Pic-Nic

When the two women in white
Came down to the lonely beach
She threw away her paintbox
And she threw away her note book
And down they sat on the sand
The tide was low
Before them the weedy rocks
Were like some herd of shabby beasts
Come down to the pool to drink
And staying there — in a kind of stupor.
Then she went off and dabbled her legs in a pool
Thinking about the colour of flesh under water
And she crawled into a dark cave
And sat there thinking about her childhood
Then they came back to the beach
And flung themselves down on their bellies
Hiding their heads in their arms
They looked like two swans.

Arrival

I seem to spend half my life arriving at strange hotels —
And asking if I may go to bed immediately.
And would you mind filling my hot water bottle
Thank you that is delicious.
No, I shan't require anything more —
The strange door shuts upon the stranger
And then I slip down in the sheets
Waiting for the shadows to come out of the corners
And spin a slow, slow web
Over the ugliest wallpaper of all.

Dame Seule

She is little and grey
With a black velvet band round her hair
False teeth
And skinny little hands coming out of frills
Like the frills on cutlets.
As I passed her room one morning
I saw her worked comb and brush bag
And her Common Prayer book
On the frilled table — —
And when she goes to the 'Ladies'
For some obscure reason she wears a little shawl.
At the dinner table, smiling brightly —
This is the first time I have ever travelled alone
And stayed by myself in a strange hotel
But my husband does not mind —
As it is so Very Quiet.
Of course if it were a *gay place*
And she draws in her chin
And the bead chain rises and falls
Upon her vanished bosom.

The Butterfly

What a day to be born!
And what a place!
Cried the flowers.
'Mais, tu as de la chance, ma chere!'
said the wild geranium
Who was very travelled.
The campions, the bluebells
The daisies and buttercups
The bright little eyebright and the white nettle flower
And a thousand others
All were there to greet her —
And growing so high — so high
Right up to the sky, thought the butterfly,
On either side of a little lane.
Only, my dear, breathed an old snail
Who was hugging the underside of a dock leaf
Dont attempt to cross over.
Keep to this side —
The other side is just the same as this
Believe me — just the same flowers — just the same greeness.
Stay where you are and have your little flutter in Peace —
That was enough for the butterfly.
What an idea! Never to go out into the open?
Never to venture forth?
To live, creeping up and down this side.
Her wings quivered with scorn.
Really, said she, I am not a snail!
And away she flew.
But just at that moment a dirty looking dog
Its mean tail between its legs
Came loping down the lane.
It just glanced aside at the butterfly — did not bite
Just gave a feeble snap and ran further.
But she was dead.

Little fleck of cerise and black
She lay in the dust.
Everybody was sorry except the Bracken —
Which never cares about anything, one way or the other.

Fairy Tale

Now folds the Tree of Day its perfect flowers,
And every bloom becomes a bud again,
Shut and sealed up against the golden showers
Of bees that hover in the velvet hours . . .
    Now a strain
Wild and mournful blown from shadow towers,
Echoed from shadow ships upon the foam,
Proclaims the Queen of Night.
    From their bowers
The dark Princesses fluttering, wing their flight
To their old Mother, in her huge old home.

Covering Wings

Love! Love! Your tenderness,
Your beautiful, watchful ways
Grasp me, fold me, cover me;
I lie in a kind of daze,
Neither asleep nor yet awake,
Neither a bud nor flower.
Brings to-morrow
Joy or sorrow,
The black or the golden hour?

Love! Love! You pity me so!
Chide me, scold me — cry,
'Submit — submit! You must not fight!'
What may I do, then — die?
But, oh — my horror of quiet beds!
How can I longer stay!
'One to be ready,
Two to be steady,
Three to be off and away!'

Darling heart — your gravity!
Your sorrowful, mournful gaze —
'Two bleached roads lie under the moon,
At the parting of the ways.'
But the tiny, tree-thatched, narrow lane,
Isn't it yours and mine?
The blue-bells ring
Hey, Ding-a-Ding, Ding!
And buds are thick on the vine.

Love! Love! grief of my heart!
As a tree droops over a stream
You hush me, lull me, darken me,
The shadow hiding the gleam.

Your drooping and tragical boughs of grace
Are heavy as though with rain.
Run! Run!
Into the sun!
Let us be children again.

Firelight

Playing in the fire and twilight together,
My little son and I,
Suddenly — woefully — I stoop to catch him.
'Try, mother, try!'

Old Nurse Silence lifts a silent finger:
'Hush! cease your play!'
What happened? What in that tiny moment
Flew away?

Sorrowing Love

And again the flowers are come
And the light shakes
And no tiny voice is dumb
And a bud breaks
On the humble bush and the proud restless tree.
Come with me!

Look, this little flower is pink
And this one white.
Here's a pearl cup for your drink,
Here's for your delight
A yellow one, sweet with honey,
Here's fairy money
Silver bright
Scattered over the grass
As we pass.

Here's moss. How the smell of it lingers
On my cold fingers.
You shall have no moss. Here's a frail
Hyacinth, deathly pale.
Not for you. Not for you.
And the place where they grew
You must promise me not to discover
My sorrowful lover!
Shall we never be happy again?
Never again play?
In vain — in vain!
Come away!

A Little Girl's Prayer

Grant me the moment, the lovely moment
That I may lean forth to see
The other buds, the other blooms,
The other leaves on the tree:

That I may take into my bosom
The breeze that is like his brother,
But stiller, lighter, whose faint laughter
Echoes the joy of the other.

Above on the blue and white cloud-spaces
There are small clouds at play.
I watch their remote, mysterious play-time
In the other far-away.

Grant I may hear the small birds singing
The song that the silence knows . . .
(The Light and the Shadow whisper together,
The lovely moment grows,

Ripples into the air like water
Away and away without sound,
And the little girl gets up from her praying
On the cold ground.)

Secret Flowers

Is love a light for me? A steady light,
A lamp within whose pallid pool I dream
Over old love-books? Or is it a gleam,
A lantern coming towards me from afar
Down a dark mountain? Is my love a star?
Ah me! so high above — so coldly bright!

The fire dances. Is my love a fire
Leaping down the twilight ruddy and bold?
Nay, I'd be frightened of him. I'm too cold
For quick and eager loving. There's a gold
Sheen on these flower petals as they fold
More truly mine, more like to my desire.

The flower petals fold. They are by the sun
Forgotten. In a shadowy wood they grow
Where the dark trees keep up a to-and-fro
Shadowy waving. Who will watch them shine
When I have dreamed my dream? Ah, darling mine!
Find them, gather them for me one by one.

Sunset

A beam of light was shaken out of the sky
On to the brimming tide, and there it lay
Palely tossing like a creature condemned to die
Who has loved the bright day.

'Ah, who are these that wing through the shadowy air'
She cries, in agony. 'Are they coming for me?'
The big waves croon to her: 'Hush now! There — now —
    there!'
There is nothing to see.

But her white arms lift to cover her shining head
And she presses close to the waves to make herself small.
On their listless knees the beam of light lies dead
And the birds of shadow fall.

Old-Fashioned Widow's Song

She handed me a gay bouquet
Of roses pulled in the rain,
Delicate beauties frail and cold —
Could roses heal my pain?

She smiled: 'Ah, c'est un triste temps!'
I laughed and answered 'Yes,'
Pressing the roses in my palms.
How could the roses guess?

She sang 'Madame est seule?' Her eye
Snapped like a rain-washed berry.
How could the solemn roses tell
Which of us was more merry?

She turned to go: she stopped to chat;
'Adieu,' at last she cried.
'Mille mercis pour ces jolies fleurs!' . . .
At that the roses died.

The petals drooped, the petals fell,
The leaves hung crisped and curled.
And I stood holding my dead bouquet
In a dead world.

The New Husband

Some one came to me and said
Forget, forget that you've been wed
Who's your man to leave you be
Ill and cold in a far country
Who's the husband — who's the stone
Could leave a child like you alone.

You're like a leaf caught in the wind
You're like a lamb that's left behind.
When all the flock has pattered away
You're like a pitiful little stray
Kitten that I'd put in my vest
You're like a bird that's fallen from nest.

We've none of us too long to live
Then take me for your man and give
Me all the Keys to all your fears
And let me kiss away these tears
Creep close to me. I mean no harm
My darling. Let me make you warm.

I had received that very day
A letter from the Other to say
That in six months — he hoped — no longer
I would be so much better and stronger
That he would close his books and come
With radiant looks to bear me home.

Ha! Ha! Six months, six weeks, six hours
Among these glittering palms and flowers
With Melancholy at my side
For my old nurse and for my guide
Despair — and for my footman Pain —
I'll never see my home again.

Said my new husband: Little dear
It's time we were away from here
In the road below there waits my carriage
Ready to drive us to our marriage
Within my home the feast is spread
And the maids are baking the bridal bread.

I thought with grief upon that other
But then why should he aught discover
Save that I pined away and died?
So I became the stranger's bride
And every moment however fast
It flies — we live as 'twere our last!

Et Après

When her last breath was taken
And the old miser death had shaken
The last, last glim from her eyes
He retired
And to the world's surprise
Wrote these inspired, passion-fired
Poems of Sacrifice!
The world said:
If she had not been dead
(And burièd)
He'd never have written these.
She was hard to please.
They're better apart
Now the stone
Has rolled away from his heart
Now he's come into his own
Alone.

He wrote

Darling Heart if you would make me
Happy, you have found the way.
Write me letters. How they shake me
Thrill me all the common day

With our love. I hear your laughter
Little laughs! I see your look
'They Lived Happy Ever After'
As you close the faery book.

Work's been nothing but a pleasure
Every silly little word
Dancing to some elfin measure
Piped by a small chuckling bird.

All this love — as though I've tasted
Wine too rare for human food —
I have dreamed away and wasted
Just because the news was good.

Where's the pain of counting money
When my little queen is there
In the parlour eating honey
Beautiful beyond compare!

How I love you! You are better.
Does it matter — being apart?
Oh, the love that's in this letter
Feel it, beating like a heart.

Beating out — 'I do adore you'
Now and to Eternity
See me as I stand before you
Happy as you'd have me be.

Don't be sad and don't be lonely
Drive away those awful fears
When they come remember only
How I've suffered these two years.

Darling heart if you must sorrow
Think: 'my pain must be his pain.'
Think: 'He will be sad tomorrow'
And then — make me smile again.

The Ring

But a tiny ring of gold
Just a link
Wear it, and your heart is sold
. . . Strange to think!

Till it glitters on your hand
You are free
Shall I cast it on the sand
In the sea?

Which was Judas' greatest sin
Kiss or gold?
Love must end where sales begin
I am told.

We will have no ring, no kiss
To deceive.
When you hear the serpent hiss
Think of Eve.

Winter Bird

My bird, my darling,
Calling through the cold of afternoon —
Those round, bright notes,
Each one so perfect
Shaken from the other and yet
Hanging together in flashing clusters!
'The small soft flowers and the ripe fruit
All are gathered.
It is the season now of nuts and berries
And round, bright, flashing drops
In the frozen grass.'

The Wounded Bird

In the wide bed
Under the green embroidered quilt
With flowers and leaves always in soft motion
She is like a wounded bird resting on a pool.

The hunter threw his dart
And hit her breast,
Hit her but did not kill.
Oh, my wings, lift me — lift me
I am not dreadfully hurt!
Down she dropped and was still.

Kind people come to the edge of the pool with baskets
'Of course what the poor bird wants is plenty of food!'
Their bags and pockets are crammed almost to bursting
With dinner scrapings and scraps from the servants' lunch.
Oh! how pleased they are to be really *giving*!
'In the past, you know you know, you were always so
    fly-away.
So seldom came to the windowsill, so rarely
Shared the delicious crumbs thrown into the yard.
Here is a delicate fragment and here a tit-bit
As good as new. And here's a morsel of relish
And cake and bread and bread and bread and bread.'

At night — in the wide bed
With the leaves and flowers
Gently weaving in the darkness
She is like a wounded bird at rest on a pool.
Timidly, timidly she lifts her head from her wing.
In the sky there are two stars
Floating — shining —
Oh, waters — do not cover me!
I would look long and long at those beautiful stars!
O my wings — lift me — lift me
I am not so dreadfully hurt . . .

Notes

The numerous textual variants from Murry's edition of *Poems by Katherine Mansfield*, 1923, and the slightly enlarged edition of 1930, derive either from the manuscripts of the poems, or from the text published in periodicals during KM's lifetime. The reader can assume that manuscripts for the majority of poems published in *Rhythm*, the *Athenaeum,* or other journals do not survive, and that the manuscripts which are available are very largely for those poems that KM did not attempt to publish. Exceptions to this are mentioned in the Notes.

Most of the manuscript poems used or referred to in this edition are held in the Alexander Turnbull Library, Wellington, and I have not spelled this out on every occasion. When I have followed a manuscript held by either the Newberry Library, Chicago, or the Humanities Research Centre, the University of Texas at Austin, this is indicated in the text. These three libraries kindly allow the use of their material.

The following books are referred to in the notes:

Alpers: *The Life of Katherine Mansfield*, Antony Alpers (London, 1982)
CLKM: Collected Letters of Katherine Mansfield, edited Vincent O'Sullivan and Margaret Scott, vol. I (Oxford, 1984), vol. II (Oxford, 1987).
Journal: Journal of Katherine Mansfield, Definitive Edition, edited John Middleton Murry (London, 1954).
LJMM: Letters of Katherine Mansfield to John Middleton Murry, edited John Middleton Murry (London, 1951).

p. 1 *'This is my world'*. Untitled by KM, these verses were given to a school friend at Queen's College, London, in 1903. Across the top of the manuscript there is the line 'K — —, Kathleen, Käthe, Kass, K. Kath, ~~Cass~~.' Manuscript from the Newberry Library.

p. 2 *'The Students' Room'*. Written at Queen's College, the manuscript is dated 2 March 1906.

p. 2 *'Vignette — Through the Autumn afternoon'*. Entitled simply 'Vignette', and dated '4 v 07'. The library in the first line is probably the Parliamentary Library in Wellington, where KM frequently read. Manuscript from the Newberry Library.

During 1907 KM worked on a book of children's verses, which

were to be illustrated by her artist friend Edith Bendall. The plan was abandoned when the friendship cooled, but Murry included twenty-two of these slight pieces in *Poems* 1923. '*A Day in Bed*' was KM's first published poem, appearing in the Australian journal the *Lone Hand* on 1 October 1909. '*The Candle Fairy*' is also printed here for the relevance of its Freudian possibilities to similar imagery in *The Aloe* and *Prelude* many years later.

A Day in Bed

I wish I had not got a cold;
   The wind is big and wild;
I wish that I was very old,
   Not just a little child.

Somehow the day is very long,
   Just keeping here alone.
I do not like the big wind's song,
   He's growling for a bone.

I'm sitting up, and Nurse has made
   Me wear a woolly shawl —
I wish I was not so afraid:
   It's horrid to be small.

It really feels quite like a day
   Since I have had my tea;
P'raps everybody's gone away,
   And just forgotten me.

And, oh, I cannot go to sleep,
   Although I am in bed;
The wind keeps going 'creepy creep'
   And waiting to be fed.

The Candle Fairy

The candle is a fairy house
That's smooth and round and white
And Mother carries it about
Whenever it is night.

Right at the top a fairy lives
A lovely yellow one
And if you blow a little bit
It has all sorts of fun.

It bows and dances by itself
In such a clever way
And then it stretches very tall
"Well, *it* grows fast" you say.

The little chimney of the house
Is black and really sweet —
And there the candle fairy stands
Though you can't see its feet.

And when the dark is very big
And you've been having dreams
Then Mother brings the candle in
How friendly like it seems!

It's only just for Mothers that
The candle fairy comes;
And if you play with it, it bites
Your fingers and your thumbs.

But still you love it very much
This candle fairy, dear
Because, at night, it always means
That Mother's very near.

pp. 4-6   *'Vignettes'*. These were published in the Australian *Native Companion* on 1 October 1907. The editor E. J. Brady felt they owed rather too much to Oscar Wilde, and KM replied on 23 September: 'I am sorry that they resemble their illustrious relatives to so marked an extent — and assure you — they feel very much my own — This style of work absorbs me, at present — but — well — it cannot be said that anything you have of mine is "cribbed" — — — Frankly — I hate plagiarism.' (*CLKM*, I, p. 26.)

p. 8 *'Silhouettes'*. In the *Native Companion*, 1 November 1907.

p. 9 *'In the Botanical Gardens'*. In the *Native Companion*, 2 December 1907, under the pseudonym 'Julian Mark'.

p. 11 *'Vignette — Westminster Cathedral'*. Written for Vere Bartrick-Baker, a friend at Queen's College, after KM's return to New Zealand. From a typed copy, Alexander Turnbull Library.

p. 12 *'Vignette — Summer in Winter'*. 'Carlotta' was a name used for Maata Mahupuku, a Maori friend with whom KM was infatuated. From a typed copy, Alexander Turnbull Library. A manuscript draft is dated 9.11.07.

p. 14 *'Leves Amores'*. The Thistle Hotel was rather a humble public hotel in Thorndon, and the social nuances of the piece remain obscure. KM wrote of it near the end of 1907, 'I can't think how I wrote it — it's partly a sort of dream.' (*CLKM*, p. 34.) The title of 'casual loves', as well as the imagery of vines, derives from Arthur Symons' 'Leves Amores' in *London Nights* 1896. From a typed copy, Newberry Library.

p. 16 *'In the Rangitaiki Valley'*. Presumably written about 20 November 1907, when a camping party KM travelled with in the centre of the North Island camped overnight at Rangitaiki.

p. 17 *'Vignette — By the Sea'*. From a typed copy, Alexander Turnbull Library. A manuscript draft is dated 'February' 1908. Much of this is similar to a notebook entry in the *Journal*, pp. 9–10.

p. 18 Study: *'The Death of a Rose'*. Published in the *Triad*, a Dunedin-based magazine 1 July 1908.

p. 19 *'Why Love is Blind'*. Written at a Wellington party where violets were the theme, and published in the social column of the *New Zealand Free Lance*, 20 June 1908. KM takes her four-line form from Robert Herrick's flower poems.

p. 19 *'The Winter Fire'*. Sent with a letter to Garnet Trowell, 2 November 1908.

p. 21 *'November'*. Originally entitled *'October'*, and published the next year in the 'Table Talk' column, the *Daily News*, 3 November 1909.

p. 22 *'Revelation'*. Dated '4 XII 08'. After her return to England in

August 1908, KM began an affair with Garnet Trowell, a young musician whose father had taught her the cello in Wellington. Towards the end of the year she wrote a considerable amount of verse, much of it posted to her lover. (See *CLKM*, pp. 81-86.) Manuscript from the Newberry Library.

p. 23 *'The Trio'*. Dated '9 XII 08'. Manuscript from the Newberry Library.

p. 25 *'Vignette — I look out through the window'*. Manuscript from the Newberry Library entitled 'Vignette' and dated '11 XII 08'.

p. 26 *'Spring Wind in London'*. Dated by Murry as 1909.

pp. *'The Arabian Shawl', 'Sleeping Together', 'The Quarrel'*. All were
27-9 written from KM's relationship with Garnet Trowell. Their tone seems rather more assured than the verses she sent him with her letters at the end of 1908, and may date from rather later. Text from *Poems*, 1923.

p. 30 *'To Stanislaw Wyspiansky'*. KM wrote her elegy on the Polish playwright artist and patriot (1868-1907) during the time she spent at Wörishen in Bavaria, June — December 1909. There she became friendly with Floryan Sobieniowski, a journalist and translator, who encouraged her interest in Slavic literature and began to teach her Polish during the time they were romantically attached. His translation of her poem was published in Warsaw in *Gazety Poniedziakowey* (*Monday Newspaper*) on 26 December 1910, although it did not appear in English until the London bookseller, Bernard Rota, brought out a small limited edition in 1938. The present text is taken from that edition. For a fuller placing of the work see Jeffrey Myers, 'Katherine Mansfield's "To Stanislaw Wyspiansky"', *Modern Fiction Studies*, Autumn vol. 23, no. 4, (1978), pp. 337-41.

p. 31 *'Loneliness'*. Alpers, p.105, places this as being written during KM's brief return to her husband George Bowden in early 1910, and sparking a quarrel between them when he suggested 'Solitude' as a less pessimistic title. Published in the *New Age*, 26 May 1910.

pp. *'The Sea Child', 'The Opal Dream Cave', 'Sea'*. These three poems
32-3

written at Rottingdean during KM's convalescence after an operation, March — June 1910. The first was published in *Rhythm*, June 1912, the others in *Rhythm*, December 1912.

p. 34 *'Along the Gray's Inn Road'*. A. R. Orage, editor of the *New Age* and now as hostile to KM as formerly he had been friendly, printed as a letter to the Editor what presumably was submitted as a prose poem, 5 October 1911.

p. 34 *'The Secret'*. Inscribed on the fly-leaf of *Light on the Path*, a 'small book of occult wisdom' in 1912. 'It was a very rare thing for us to speak of our relationship.' (Ida Baker, *The Memories of LM*, (1971) pp. 68-9.) Manuscript from the Humanities Research Centre, Texas.

p. 35 *'Very Early Spring'*, *'The Awakening River'*. Both published in *Rhythm*, Spring 1912, signed Katherine Mansfield, but claiming to be translations from an imaginary Russian, Boris Petrovsky. The second poem provoked A. R. Orage, who attacked *Rhythm* in his *New Age*, 19 April 1912, to speak of 'pampering pretty feelings until the very rivers seemed to lie in sexual ecstasy'. (See Alpers, p. 137.)

p. 36 *'The Earth-Child in the Grass'*. Under the name of Boris Petrovsky, in *Rhythm*, September 1912.

p. 37 *'To God the Father'*. Again claiming to be a Petrovsky translation, *Rhythm*, November 1912.

p. 38 *'Floryan nachdenklich'*. German for 'Floryan — pensive', published in the Wellington daily, the *Dominion*, 3 March 1913.

p. 39 *'Jangling Memory'*. By Boris Petrovsky, *Rhythm*, January 1913.

p. 40 *'There Was a Child Once'*. By Boris Petrovsky, *Rhythm*, March 1913. According to Ida Baker the poem concerned KM's friendship with William Orton, whose autobiographical novel *The Last Romantic*, 1937, includes otherwise lost extracts from KM's letters and notebooks.

p. 41 *'Sea Song'*. Under Mansfield's own name, *Rhythm*, March 1913.

p. 42 *'The Meeting'*. Written on 27 March 1914, the poem records Ida Baker's leaving for Rhodesia for two years. (See Alpers pp. 165-6.)

p. 43 *'Countrywomen'*, *'Stars'*. The titles for both supplied by Murry, who gives their date as 1914.

p. 45 *'Deaf House Agent'*. Printed by Murry in the *Journal*, pp. 60-1, as well as in *Poems*, 1923, and dated by him as July 1914. The reference to looking for a place in the country makes September more likely.

p. 46 *'Villa Pauline'*. In *Poems*, 1923, Murry placed these and the next six poems as a group, 'Poems at the Villa Pauline'. His introductory note, p. xiii, recorded that with the exception of the sonnet to her brother, they 'were written in curious circumstances. Villa Pauline was a four-roomed cottage on the shore of the Mediterranean where we lived in 1916. [November 1915 — February 1916.] For the whole of one week we made a practice of sitting together at a very small table in the kitchen and writing verses on a single theme which we had chosen.' He does not mention that the verses made no pretence to being finished poems and that the manuscripts are the roughest of drafts.

p. 50 *'The Town Between the Hills'*. Perhaps Christina Rossetti's 'Goblin Market' might claim a remote ancestry for this occasional piece.

p. 52 *'Voices of the air!'* Although Murry says, *Poems* 1923, pp. xiii-iv, 'It seems to me now almost miraculous that so exquisite a poem … should have been thus composed,' it is perhaps more interesting as an example of his editorial method. He printed only four of the poem's six stanzas, implying a completed poem which in fact was not the case, the manuscript trailing off into a rapid and much cancelled scrawl. The last two stanzas might be transcribed:

> The insect hanging upon a stem
> And the beads of water dropping along

The mosses, the big rocks and diadem
And its infinite silent song.

The silent song so faint so rare
That the heart must not beat
Nor the quick blood run
To hear the inspired voices of the air.

p. 53 *'Sanary'*. A fishing village close to Bandol, towards Menton.

p. 54 *'To L. H. B. (1894-1915)'*. Leslie Heron Beauchamp, KM's only brother, was killed at Ploegsteert Wood, near Armentières, on 7 October 1915, while serving as a lieutenant in the South Lancashire Regiment.

p. 54 *'Butterflies'*, called 'Butterfly Laughter' in *Poems* 1923, as Murry used another manuscript. This and the next nine poems are from fair copies written on identical paper and were clipped together as a group. The subject and tone of *'The Gulf'*, as well as Ida Baker's confirmation, place this as a poem written after her brother's death, and it is likely that the others come from the same time. As she noted in January 1916, 'I want to write poetry. I feel always trembling on the brink of poetry. The almonds, the birds, the little wood where you are, the flowers you do not see, the open window out of which I lean & dream that you are against my shoulder.' (*Journal*, p. 94.) This would place them much later than Murry's date in *Poems* 1923, where they are given as 1909-1910.

p. 56 *'The Grandmother'*. Not published with the rest of this group in *Poems* 1923 although clearly a part of them.

p. 61 *'Night Scented Stock'*. Set at Lady Ottoline Morrell's Garsington Manor near Oxford, the poem partly attempts what KM projected in August 1917 as a story set in the house's famous garden. (See *CLKM*, I, p. 325.) In part it is also a pastiche of mannerisms she took from T. S. Eliot's recent *Prufrock and other Observations*, which already KM had satirically drawn on when writing to

Lady Ottoline soon after giving a reading from the volume at Garsington the previous June. (See *CLKM*, I, pp. 312-13.) 'Is the moon a virgin or a harlot', a memory from Oscar Wilde's *Salomé*. Manuscript from the Humanities Research Centre, Texas.

p. 63 *'Now I am a Plant, a Weed'*, *'Out in the Garden'*. Both dated by Murry as 1917. Manuscripts from the Humanities Research Centre, Texas, the roughest of first drafts.

p. 65 *'Strawberries and the Sailing Ship'*. Written at Looe during May — June 1918. She later recast this and other poems from the same time into prose paragraphs which Murry included in the *Journal*, although he did not consider the verses for *Poems* 1923.

p. 66 *'Malade'*. The prose version entitled *Pulmonary Tuberculosis, Journal*, p. 139.

p. 66 *'Pic-Nic'*. Under the same title in prose, *Journal*, p. 140, with the word *she* italicized throughout.

p. 67 *'Arrival'*. The title changed by Murry to *'Hotels'* in the prose paragraph, *Journal*, p. 139.

p. 67 *'Dame Seule'*. The prose version was in the *Journal*, pp. 140-1. Other *Journal* entries at this time such as *Remembrance*, p. 141, recalling the Lawrences and foxgloves, may also have begun as poems.

p. 68 *'The Butterfly'*. Mentioned in a letter to Murry, 30 May 1918.

p. 69 *'Fairy Tale'*. By 'Elizabeth Stanley', the *Athenaeum*, 18 April 1919. The name which she took from her paternal grandmother was used with all KM verses published in the *Athenaeum*.

p. 70 *'Covering Wings'*, *'Firelight'*. Both published in the *Athenaeum*, 25 April 1919.

p. 72 *'Sorrowing Love'*. The *Athenaeum*, 23 May 1919. Manuscript from the Newberry Library.

p. 73 *'A Little Girl's Prayer'*. The *Athenaeum*, 4 July 1919.

p. 74 *'Secret Flowers'*. The *Athenaeum*, 22 July 1919. The one *Athenaeum* poem that Murry did not include in *Poems* 1923 or 1930.

p. 75 *'Sunset', 'Old-Fashioned Widow's Song'*. Both in the *Athenaeum*, 9 January 1920, and both added by Murry in *Poems* 1930.

p. 77 *'The New Husband'*. KM sent Murry this poem with a letter from Ospedaletti on 4 December 1919, during a time between them that was troubled by money, Murry's friendships with other women, KM's health, and general apprehension about their future. Her postscript read 'Darling please keep all these verses for me in the file — will you? I'll polish them up one day and have them published.' (*LJMM*, p. 426.) The fact that she signed it with her pseudonym 'Elizabeth Stanley' perhaps made her believe it was sufficiently distanced not to distress Murry; but it did, extremely.

pp. *'Et Après', 'He wrote'*. Both were sent with the same letter. Murry
78-9 did not include any of these in his editions of the *Poems*, but he did publish 'The New Husband' in *LJMM*, p. 427, and the other two in the *Journal*, pp. 181-2.

p. 80 *'The Ring'*. An obvious pastiche of Robert Browning's 'A Woman's Last Word', a poem that carried particular significance for KM and Murry, and which she mentions in a letter to him in mid-December 1919. (*LJMM* p. 448.)

p. 81 *'Winter Bird'*. Probably written during KM's time at the Chalet des Sapins, Montana-sur-Sierre, where she lived from June 1921 to January 1922. In the *Scrapbook of Katherine Mansfield* 1939, p. 130.

p. 82 *'The Wounded Bird'*. Written at the Hôtel Château Belle Vue, Sierre, Montana, during July 1922, where with injury and confinement on her mind KM also wrote the last of her stories, 'The Canary'.

Index of titles and first lines

Titles are in *italics*; first lines in roman.